ONE PEACE

True Stories of Young Activists

Written and illustrated by JANET WILSON

ORCA BOOK PUBLISHERS

Library and Archives Canada Cataloguing in Publication

Wilson, Janet, 1952-
One peace / written and illustrated by Janet Wilson.

ISBN 978-1-55143-892-4

1. Peace--Juvenile literature. 2. Pacifists--Juvenile literature.
3. Children and peace--Juvenile literature. I. Title.

JZ5535.W54 2008   j327.1'72   C2008-902688-8

First published in the United States, 2008
Library of Congress Control Number: 2008927399

Summary: World peace is attainable through positive action. Examples are taken from the lives of child crusaders for peace.

Orca Book Publishers gratefully acknowledges the support for its publishing programs provided by the following agencies: the Government of Canada through the Book Publishing Industry Development Program and the Canada Council for the Arts, and the Province of British Columbia through the BC Arts Council and the Book Publishing Tax Credit.

Cover artwork by Janet Wilson
Design by Teresa Bubela

ORCA BOOK PUBLISHERS
PO Box 5626, STN. B
VICTORIA, BC CANADA
V8R 6S4

ORCA BOOK PUBLISHERS
PO Box 468
CUSTER, WA USA
98240-0468

www.orcabook.com
Printed and bound in China.

11 10 09 08 • 4 3 2 1

One Peace: True Stories of Young Activists *is dedicated to young peacemakers*
who can be the change they wish to see in the world.

Individually they appear to be like snowflakes, small and fragile,
but see what happens when they come together...

Everywhere in the world, people want **peace**.

"I am the Peacemaker. I plant the Great Tree of Peace..."

The White Roots of Peace have spread out to cover the world. Anyone who obeys the Great Law of Peace, based on liberty, dignity and harmony, may trace the roots to their source and take shelter beneath the Tree.

—Six Nations oral tradition

The boy stood by the fire as the women prepared the morning meal. With chin held high, he said, "The Creator has spoken to me in a dream." His grandmother and mother paused, giving the boy their full attention. "I have been chosen to stop wars and killing among nations." Eight years before, the boy's unmarried Huron mother had the same dream: the baby she carried would bring peace to the world. Her mother was angry and didn't believe her daughter's story. As the child grew, they noticed that the boy was extraordinarily kind, with a unique ability to see all points of view. Now the grandmother was certain that her daughter had spoken the truth.

The Creator instructed the boy to build a white stone canoe. When it was finished, he set out on his journey to spread the Great Law of Peace and unite the warring Indian Nations. From then on, he was known only as the Peacemaker.

OnE PeAcE

"My religion is simple. My religion is kindness."
—Dalai Lama, Tibetan Buddist spiritual leader

"I was in a neighbor's basement. We were there because they fired rockets at us. It was bad in the basement. It was dangerous. It was cold and dark and damp. We were there for a long time. One small girl went deaf because of the shelling. I was scared."
—Saidat, 10, Chechnya

For millennia our ancestors roamed the land, using their strong natural instincts to hunt and gather the necessities of life. Violent skirmishes between tribes occurred over acts that threatened their survival. Over ten thousand years ago, people who lived in fertile lands began to farm and settle in communities. Farmers became more prosperous than their hunter-gatherer neighbors; this inequality led to clashes. The first soldiers armed themselves to protect their community. Later, wars were waged to acquire more land or resources. When wars began to be fought not out of necessity, but to protect or impose a belief system, soldiers began to be forced, or paid, to serve in armies. Then came another worldwide phenomenon—prophets of peace, such as the Peacemaker, who denounced war and encouraged people to love their neighbors and live in peace.

The progression of arms throughout history. As civilization developed, so did weapons of war. Soldiers fought hand-to-hand with clubs and spears, and later with muskets and cannons. With the invention of weapons of mass destruction in the twentieth century, the face of war changed dramatically. In modern wars the majority of casualties are inflicted upon innocent civilians.

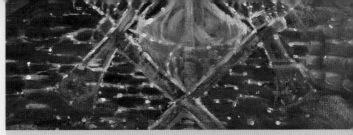

"There is no trust more sacred than the one the world holds with children." —Kofi Annan, former secretary-general of the United Nations

September 21 is the **International Day of Peace**. To join the worldwide movement to create a culture of peace and to find out what you can do to support peace and nonviolence, go to **www.internationaldayofpeace.org**.

Did you know that in the last decade:

- 2,000,000 children were killed in armed conflict
- 10,000,000 traumatized
- 2,000,000 displaced within their own countries
- 250,000 displaced outside their home countries
- 8,000-10,000 killed or maimed by landmines[1]

Donations to UNICEF provide long-term help for services that promote the health and well-being of children in developing and war-torn countries. To learn more about how to donate, go to **www.unicef.org**.[2]

The Peacemaker asked his followers to "bury their hatchets" for peace beneath the Great Tree of Peace.

Dream of Peace

Peace in our country,
A truce in our land,
Harmony in the world,
All war banned.
I live in Dungannon,
I've never known peace,
I'm tired of the choppers,
Soldiers and police.

I'm tired of the sirens,
The town's like a cage,
I wish there was peace,
I'm eleven years of age.

Laragh Cullen, 11
Dungannon, County Tyrone, Ireland

"I know there is a war going on but I don't know why. I hear about bombs on the television, about bombs going off in shops and on buses, and it makes me afraid. What are my three wishes? I want to be an artist. I want to dance. And I want to be old." —Three Wishes: Palestinian & Israeli Children Speak, Deb Ellis (House of Anansi Press)

Children don't start **wars.**

"Politics are conducted by grown-ups, but I think we young would do it better. We certainly wouldn't have chosen war. The politicians really are playing, which is why us kids are not playing. We are living in fear, we are suffering, we are not enjoying the sun and flowers. We are not enjoying our childhood. WE ARE CRYING." —Zlata Filipović, 12, Yugoslavia[3]

Saturday, July 17, 1993

Dear Mimmy,

Suddenly, someone is using the ugly powers of war to pull and drag me away from the peaceful and lovely shores of my childhood. I feel like a swimmer who was made to enter the cold water against her will. I feel shocked, sad, unhappy and frightened, and I wonder where they are forcing me to go. I used to rejoice at each new day—at the sun, at playing, at songs. I have less and less strength to keep swimming in these cold waters. So take me back to the shores of my childhood, where I was warm, happy and content, like all the children whose childhood and the right to enjoy it are now being destroyed.

Your Zlata

"How wonderful it is that nobody need wait a single moment before starting to improve the world."
—Anne Frank (1929–1945)

"There is no safe place for children. We are always living in fear." —Sudanese refugee, Africa

Zlata Filipovic was inspired by the book *Anne Frank: The Diary of a Young Girl*[4] to write about her own experience during the Bosnian War in 1992: *Zlata's Diary: A Child's Life in Wartime Sarajevo*. Zlata continues to work for peace.

For children in the developed world, home is a symbol of love, warmth and security. Every day, children whose lives are in danger flee their homes with only the things they can carry. They become refugees and live in camps. Their home, culture, family and safety become a fading memory.

In 2007, there were 10 million official refugees, but the United Nations estimated the real number of stateless persons was closer to 15 million across the globe, 44 percent of whom are children.

CHILDREN, STOP BEHAVING LIKE ADULTS!

"United, the children can make this world a very sweet and lovely place to live. All the children of the world should raise their voice and request their parents and elders to refrain from any kind of terrorism and hatred."
—Pratik Kharel, 13, Nepal

There has been an ongoing crisis of insecurity since 2003 in Sudan's Darfur region. The estimated 1.7 million children in refugee camps have constantly faced violence, severe food shortages and disease. Many are orphans. Although most camps and surrounding towns now have basic social services, provided largely by humanitarian groups, there are still some 1.2 million children who haven't been reached.

"I believe ordinary people, especially young people, can make a difference in bringing a better life to Darfur's children." Ronan Farrow (left) speaks with a woman in the Abu Shouk camp for displaced people, near the city of El Fasher, capital of northern Darfur. Ronan and his mother, Mia Farrow, are passionate and outspoken advocates for Sudanese women and children caught up in the Darfur genocide.[5]

Kids' Guernica, Nepal
Art is a language native to all children. Kids' Guernica, inspired by Pablo Picasso's anti-war mural Guernica,[6] *is a project for children around the world to use their creativity and imagination to create murals with their own powerful messages of peace.*

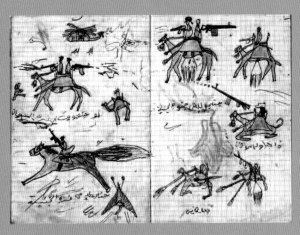

"I discovered a small group of children, caked in dust and clothed in rags, absorbed in drawing. Their bright crayons, provided by relief workers, seemed cheerful where everything is the color of sand. Then I saw the subjects of their artwork: villages burning, helicopters attacking and uniformed men with guns; bullets in midair, heads blown away. They drew no heroes. In their pictures, as in their lives, no one is there to save them."
—Ronan Farrow, UNICEF spokesperson for youth

Can children start **peace**?

"We can't change the whole world alone, but if I can teach people that if you put your hand in mine and little by little we join more hands, maybe we can construct a new world." **–Farlis Calle, 15, Colombia**

Farlis Calle was stricken with grief when her friend Jorge died. She was angry too, angry about the civil war that had plagued Colombia, South America, for six generations. During this dark time, the United Nations sent Graça Machel to investigate the impact of armed conflict on children. When she asked them to express their feelings about war, a spark in Farlis ignited what soon became a blaze. Twenty-six children organized an election to encourage the nation to listen to their plea for peace to give youth a vote for the right to life, family and freedom from abuse. Death threats almost stopped the election, but Farlis refused to quit. "You can't kill the hopes of kids!" With unwavering faith and courage, the children publicly asked the drug traffickers, guerrillas and soldiers for a cease-fire on Election Day. On October 25, 1996, nearly three million children voted for peace.

The Colombian Children's Movement for Peace founders, in Geneva to accept the Children's Nobel Prize: Mayerly Sanchez, Dilia Suarez, Juan Elias Uribe, Wilfrido Zambrano and Farlis Calle, with Desmond Tutu.

A Peace Child had an important role to play as peacemaker in the traditional culture of Papua New Guinea. When warring tribes made peace, they exchanged a baby. If the threat of conflict arose in the future, the Peace Children were sent to negotiate.

The Colombian Children's Movement for Peace (CCMP) succeeded in establishing "peace zones" in schools and parks. One year later, ten million adults voted for peace, pledging their support for the **Children's Mandate for Peace.** The CCMP was nominated twice for the **Nobel Peace Prize.**

Today, when Farlis Calle thinks about the Children's Movement for Peace, she is reminded how powerful kids are when they get together and work for their dreams.

Although Colombia still suffers through violence, thousands of children continue to volunteer to help other children become peacemakers. People remember the **Day of Tranquility** when they had peace and proved that children of war can be soldiers of peace. They still dream that one day peace will return forever.

> **"We request to all the adults of all the countries in the world:**
> Peace in the world.
> Peace in our countries.
> Peace in our homes.
> Peace in our hearts."
> —Colombian Children's Movement for Peace

> *"Children are sweet and beautiful, but we want to show adults that the role of the child must be elevated; there are acute crises in countries when children have to make up part of the solution. You say children are the future. But we are the present, a present which we all have to build together."* —Farlis Calle

David Shepherd and Travis Price, graduating students, Central Kings Rural High School, Cambridge, Nova Scotia

When David Shepherd and Travis Price heard that a new boy was bullied for wearing pink, they bought seventy-five pink tank tops for guys in the school to wear. As word spread, more students wore pink. This pink protest soon drew international attention, inspiring other schools to stage pink days, with the majority of students showing up in something pink—from feather boas to pink bicycles. The Nova Scotia government has proclaimed the second Thursday in every new school year **Stand Up Against Bullying Day.**

"The universal language of art, particularly spoken through the innocent brushstroke of a child's hand, crosses political, religious and geographic barriers."
—George Rodrigue, the International
Child Art Foundation

Peace Begins With Me

When my sister ignores me
As I'm telling her things
I get so annoyed—
She just stands there and sings!

She won't do as I do or do as I say
In even the smallest, most good-natured way.
Yet, she is my sister, yes, she is anyway
So I really must see now, I really must see,
That peace must begin with me.

When I'm playing in my fort at school
And kids pretend that I'm not there
I get so annoyed, I feel like a fool
So start to act like I just don't care.

But then I remember
That two wrongs aren't right
That playing is smarter than having a fight
It takes me a while,
But I eventually see
That peace must always begin with me.

Arianna Zimmerman, 8
Canada

FACT: Costa Rica has no army.[7]

You have the power to make peace—the power of **one**.

"The youth of the world need to be part of the solution to the world's problems. We may feel that what we are doing is just a drop in the ocean, but the ocean would be less because of that missing drop."
—Craig Kielburger, 12, Canada

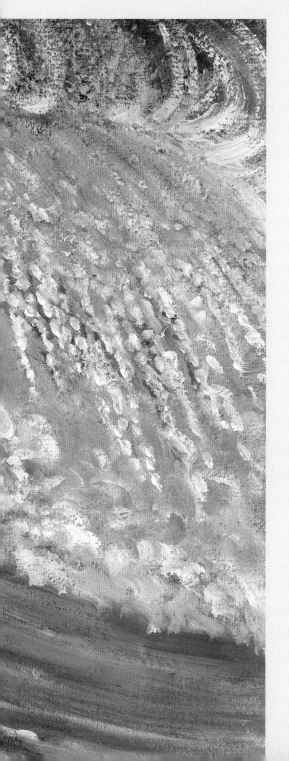

Craig Kielburger scanned the newspaper to find the comics and noticed a headline: "Boy, twelve, murdered for speaking out against child labor." Craig, also twelve, was astonished to read that Iqbal Masih was sold to pay a debt when he was four, and that he worked twelve hours a day, six days a week, chained to a loom, tying tiny knots in a carpet factory. Craig decided that he must do something to help free from abuse and exploitation the 250 million child slaves in the world. Confident that he was not too young, Craig, and eleven Canadian classmates, formed Free The Children. They gave speeches, circulated petitions and spoke to world leaders about children's rights. Within two years, they raised enough money to open schools and rehabilitation centers for victims of child labor. Free The Children, the largest network of children helping children in the world, has helped more than a million youth in over forty-five countries.

"Youth are called naïve dreamers for hoping for a world without war. Dreamers imagined the end of the slave trade, the Berlin Wall and apartheid in South Africa. If all young people became involved in a single action to promote peace, we would be unstoppable."
—Craig Kielburger

Iqbal Masih, a member of the Bonded Labor Liberation Front and the youngest winner of the international Reebok Human Rights Award. He was murdered in 1995.

Free The Children has:

- Built over 500 schools serving 50,000 children every day
- Shipped over 202,500 school and health kits
- Helped more than 505,000 families receive critical health care services
- Assisted over 22,500 women with alternative income projects so their children don't have to work

On behalf of **Free The Children (FTC)**, young people have raised money from bake sales, car washes and birthday money. FTC has received many awards, including the **World's Children's Prize for the Rights of the Child**, and been nominated three times for the **Nobel Peace Prize**. Craig Kielburger is the youngest Canadian to receive the **Order of Canada**.

"My tenth birthday was my most important birthday so far. I raised $1,100 for Free The Children in honor of all the "invisible" children around the world. These parties made me look past my own needs and helped me understand how young people could change the world for the better. Would you like to mark your next birthday with your very own Celebrate for Change campaign? FTC can help. Go to www.freethechildren.com."
—Brennan Wong, 10, Canada

Craig Kielburger observes a child laborer making bricks.

Did you know:

- Globally, 218 million children are child laborers
- 126 million of these children are engaged in hazardous work
- 73 million working children are less than ten years old
- Every year, 22,000 children die in work-related accidents
- The largest number of working children—122 million—are in the Asia-Pacific region
  (Source: UNICEF)

Me to We, by Craig and Marc Kielburger, is an international bestseller. **Me to We** philosophy is about focusing less on "Me" and more on "We"—our communities, our nation and our world as a whole. We can challenge ourselves to live a more fulfilling life by making a commitment to change the world for the better in whatever way we can, by reaching out to others and engaging in daily acts of kindness.

Thousands of candles can be lit from a single candle, and the life of the candle will not be shortened. Happiness never decreases by being shared. —Buddha, Indian philosopher and religious leader (563–483 BC)

Peace Is For All

It does not matter where you are
Whether near or whether far
If you're big or if you're small
Or if you're short or if you're tall
Or if you're young or if you're old
It does not matter what you're told
Peace is for everyone
And everything under the sun
And every age and every face
And every size and every race.

Emtithal Mahmoud, 12
Sudan/United States

The Lions International Peace Poster contest Merit Award Winner 2000–2001, painted by You Kyeong Jin, Republic of Korea.

One can **wish** for peace.

"Paper crane, I will write peace on your wings and you will fly all over the world." —**Sadako Sasaki, 12 (1943–1955), Japan**

Sadako Sasaki took the candy out of the wrapper, popped it in her mouth and pressed out all the wrinkles of the paper foil. She cut it into a square, and then she folded and creased the square gold paper with a sewing needle until a delicate origami bird perched in the palm of her hand. Sadako pulled the tail, smiling as the wings flapped. There was a Japanese legend that said someone who folded a thousand origami cranes would be granted a wish. Sadako leaned back on the pillow, closed her eyes and wished that she and this crane could fly—fly out of her hospital window and feel the breeze on her face, just as she had when she ran a race faster than any girl in her class. Then Sadako thought of the other children who had become ill and died after exposure to radiation from the atomic bomb that was dropped near her home in Hiroshima ten years before. Sadako had a greater wish—a wish for peace.

On August 6, 1945, during the Second World War, Americans dropped the first uranium atomic bomb on Hiroshima. They dropped a plutonium bomb on Nagasaki three days later. At least 105,000 people died from the mushroom-cloud explosions that rose eighteen kilometers in the air. Many survivors, like Sadako, died prematurely from radiation sickness.

The Children's Monument for Peace inscription:
Let no more children fall victim to an atomic bombing. This is our cry. This is our prayer for building peace in the world.

Sadako Sasaki died on October 25, 1955, from leukemia, a cancer of the blood. Sadako's class folded cranes for her coffin and collected the poems and letters of tribute for a book. As the news of Sadako and her cranes began to spread across Japan, more children sent origami cranes to her school. They decided to erect a statue in memory of Sadako and all children killed by the atomic bomb. Young people from all over Japan sent donations. In 1958, a sculpture of Sadako holding a paper crane, the **Children's Monument for Peace**, was erected in the Hiroshima Peace Park.

Ban the Bomb symbol, Lennon Wall, Prague

The **Ban the Bomb symbol** turned fifty on April 6, 2008. Its designer, Gerald Holtom, was highly alarmed about nuclear weapons during the Cold War and adapted the semaphore signs for N and D, standing for nuclear disarmament. The design gained popularity in the 1960s during the Vietnam War and is now an international symbol of peace.

One can **protest** for peace.

"Let our voices echo to all children of the world to express themselves through art. Art allows us to be creative, gives us inner peace and, above all, helps us develop patience. These are virtues of peace on earth."
—Philbert Tiki Yong, 12, Malaysia

The **Art Miles Project** started in a Bosnian orphanage with one bullet-riddled bedsheet that was painted by over three hundred children of different ethnic groups. The resulting artwork was such a powerful way to teach understanding and respect, the originators dreamed of adding 447 more murals of different themes to make a mile of art. Since then, many miles have been completed. Now they have another dream—to surround the Great Pyramid of Egypt.

An Art Miles mural from Syria.

An Art Miles mural from China.

Our Wish

If from above our heads missiles and
  bombs
were not being dropped but rather
  books and notebooks,
we shall be liberated from ignorance
  and prejudice,
and we shall stop fighting and live
  together in peace.

If under this ground there were not
  buried
landmines or the like but seeds of
  wheat and corn,
we shall not be suffering from starvation
  and hurt.
And we shall share everything and live
  together in peace.

Our Wish, *two verses of a peace song from Hiroshima to the world, was written by students at the Ohzu Junior Middle School in 2002. Children from around the world are invited to add verses in different languages to make a record for the longest peace song ever written.*

FACT: Alfred Nobel, the Swede who bequeathed the five Nobel Prizes, invented dynamite.

"I feel there is beauty in all places and in all cultures. It is one world and we are brothers and sisters. War destroys this beauty, war is ugly; it makes people do ugly things, it brings hatred and it scars people inside and outside." **—Sonia Azad, 8, Great Britain**

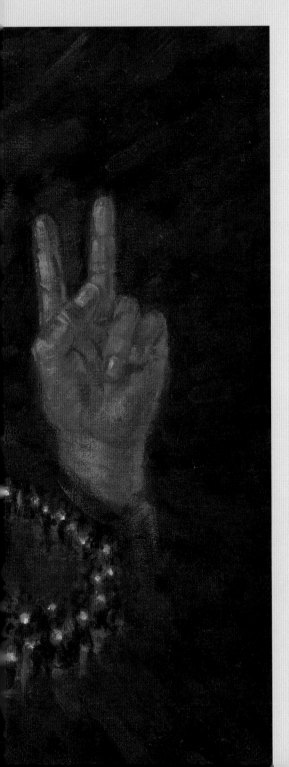

Dear Mr. Bush and Mr. Blair,

I would like to ask you questions. Please can you answer them?

What happens to the children when their Mums and Dads are killed?

What happens to the children when they see their brothers and sisters killed?

What happens to the children when they see their friends and neighbors killed?

What happens to the children when their homes and schools are bombed?

I know, Mr. Bush and Mr. Blair, that the lives of children will be destroyed if you drop bombs on Iraq.

Children must be kept safe.
No war on Iraq!
By Sonia, 8

"Do you need a child to tell you? Enough is enough. Children have the right to live in Peace!" —Sonia Azad

Since she was seven, Sonia Azad has written several letters to political leaders. The organization she helped found, **Children Against the War,** has held many peace demonstrations. Sonia has made films to give a voice to the war children of Iraq. Every year on her birthday, she organizes a candlelight vigil to speak out on their behalf.

Mohandas Gandhi was given the name Mahatma—"Great Soul"—by the people of India for peacefully leading them to independence and justice through nonviolent protests. Gandhi's belief in religious and racial tolerance inspired leaders around the world to follow his example.

"If we are to teach real peace in this world, and if we are to carry a real war against war, we shall have to begin with the children." —Mahatma Gandhi

Filipino children shout "We want peace, not war" during a protest at a Manila park.

Gandhi's birthday, October 2, is the International Day of Nonviolence. Children working as actors in the 1982 movie Gandhi *initiated the idea. In India, children dressed as Gandhi take to the streets to celebrate his birth.*

When the war in Iraq started on March 20, 2003, people in cities around the world united to form human peace signs. The V finger sign originally stood for "victory."

Peace can build a world

Peace can win a battle
Without guns or bullets.
Peace can save a nation
Without fights or speeches.

Peace can join two countries
Without roads or rails.
Peace can give a message
Without posts or mails.

Peace can bind two hearts
Without hammers or nails.
Peace can do all
War can—but peace never fails.

Priyanka Choudhury, 13
Calcutta, India

"When people think about bombing Iraq, they see a picture in their heads of Saddam Hussein or maybe soldiers with big black mustaches carrying guns. But guess what? More than half of Iraq's 24 million people are children under the age of fifteen. That's 12 million kids. Kids like me. Well, I'm almost thirteen, so some are a little older and some a lot younger, some boys instead of girls, some with brown hair, not red. So take a look at me—a good long look. Because I am what you should see in your head when you think about bombing Iraq."
—Charlotte Aldebron, 13, United States

The Tiananmen Square protests of 1989 were a series of nonviolent demonstrations in the People's Republic of China. When a column of eighteen tanks arrived on the Avenue of Eternal Peace, a lone unarmed student stood defiantly in front, halting their progress for over half an hour. Cartoon by Roopa Basu, 10, India

Painting by Hoimoboti Choudhury, 16, India, depicting bombing with candy and flowers.

One can **make a difference** for peace.

"More children need to get involved. Young people have immense power in numbers—more than we realize. Our generation could go down as the generation to end world poverty." **–Kimmie Weeks, Liberia/United States**

Kimmie Weeks drifted in and out of consciousness, stricken by the cholera that raged through the displacement camp, but no medicine was available for the ten-year-old African refugee from the Liberian civil war. Kimmie was declared dead and ordered to be placed in a mass grave. His mother refused to believe her son was dead; she beat her fists on Kimmie's chest, trying desperately to revive him. Then she saw his eyelids flutter. That night, Kimmie wondered why he had lived when so many others had died. He reflected on the horrors of his childhood—the hunger that forced him to eat roots and wild leaves, the thirst that drove him to drink infested water, and the sight of all kinds of human suffering. Kimmie decided that his life was spared to make a difference in the lives of other children. He made a vow that no child would ever go without food, water and medicine.

I Will Lay Down the Arms Now

Conscripted away from my mother and father
To shoot and murder another
I cannot go any further
With this shooting and killing that has no border.
Forgive me now if I injured your brother.
I was forced to pull the trigger
By elders who made my childhood wither.

*—Rashid Peters, 15, a youth peace
advocate, Sierra Leone*

*"Young people in the developed world have to
appreciate their blessings and extend a helping
hand to children in the developing world. I saw
children suffer and die, cut down by bullets or
preventable diseases. I saw children selling goods for
their families to survive, while thousands of others
carried guns. Each and every person, regardless
of age, can do something to save a life."*
—Kimmie Weeks

Kimmie Weeks cared for sick babies at the hospital and organized the cleanup of the debris of war. At thirteen, he established Liberia's first child-rights advocacy group. **Voices of the Future** offered peer counseling and education for former child soldiers and provided health care and recreation supplies to children. Kimmie faced assasination attempts in response to his campaign to disarm 20,000 child soldiers. He escaped to America where he founded **Youth Action International**, now in six African countries. Kimmie continues to be a passionate activist for children, women and the environment.

*In Uganda, Africa, thousands of children fled their
homes to escape being abducted for training as child
soldiers, walking miles at night to find a safe haven.
To raise awareness of these children, on October 20,
youths from around the world hold "GuluWalks."*

FACT: One out of ten soldiers
is a child.

Child soldier, Burma/Myanmar.
"My gun was as tall as me."

Forcing children to participate in war is a crime, yet at the beginning of the twenty-first century there were more than 250,000 child soldiers around the world (www.childsoldiersglobalreport.org). In war-torn areas where society has completely disintegrated, children are the most vulnerable victims. Orphaned, starving and traumatized from witnessing atrocities, they are easy targets for recruitment and kidnapping. Desperate children are given food, shelter and a sense of security or belonging; at the same time they are threatened, abused and drugged. Uneducated children are easily brainwashed. If rescued in time, many child soldiers are successfully rehabilitated through counseling and education.

War Child

I lost my father and mother in this battle.
My brothers, too, perished in this struggle.
All my life I've been hiding in the jungle.

I'm a War Child

The pain I carry is too much to handle.
Who's there please to light my candle?
Is there anyone to hear my cry?

I believe I've survived for a reason:
To tell my story, to touch lives.

Excerpted lyrics by **Emmanuel Jal**

Emmanuel Jal is an award-winning international rap artist. When he was eight, he was forced to join the rebel Sudanese People's Liberation Army to fight in a civil war for four years. Today he is fighting for peace and love.

One can **volunteer** for peace.

"Every day, I will do one thing to make peace grow like a flower. Every day, I will spend five minutes reflecting peacefully. I will help landmine survivors. I will care for and not destroy the environment. I will try to solve arguments without violence." **—Song Kosal, 13, Cambodia**

Song Kosal leaned on her crutch, trying to summon the courage to speak to the shoemaker. "Could you make me only one shoe?" The old man shook his head, waving his hand in refusal. In Cambodia, to sell only one shoe would bring him bad luck. Kosal hung her head in shame, embarrassed by the empty space below the hem of her dress. Kosal needed only one shoe. While working with her mother in the rice paddy when she was five, Kosal stepped on a hidden landmine. The explosion caused a severe injury to her right leg and it had to be amputated.

The experience filled Kosal with the determination to spread a message of peace around the world so that other children wouldn't be harmed. She founded **Youth Against War**, an organization that encourages young people to make the world a better place.

Song Kosal at the signing of the Mine Ban Treaty in Ottawa, 1997, with Jean Chrétien (right) and Kofi Annan (middle).

S ince she was twelve, Song Kosal has been speaking around the world about the need to ban landmines. The Canadian government invited her to witness the signing of the Mine Ban Treaty, in which governments committed to help mine survivors, fund mine clearance and destroy their stockpiles of mines. She was the first person to sign the Peoples' Treaty, an agreement among citizens of the world to encourage their governments to keep their promises to sign the treaty to ban landmines.

Landmines are containers of explosives that are triggered by the weight of a person, animal or vehicle. The military bury them by hand or scatter them by airplanes. In spite of treaties to ban their use, landmines continue to be manufactured and used by countries at war; an estimated one hundred million landmines remain hidden and active long after conflict has ended in the fields, roads and footpaths of one-third of the countries in the developing world.

"Sometimes I dream that I have two legs again and I run freely through the rice fields, feeling the grass under my toes. I really wish that soon my friends and I can play without danger, with no more mines in our fields." —Song Kosal

Children around the world have been active in the International Campaign to Ban Landmines, as in this demonstration from Paris. In 1995, two hundred Austrian children delivered to their parliament six tons of shoes filled with hand-drawn butterflies to symbolize the unneeded shoes of amputee survivors.

Every twenty-two minutes, one person somewhere in the world is killed or injured by a landmine. In 2006, according to the 2007 Landmine Moniter Report, 5,751 casualties were reported in sixty-eight countries and areas; three-quarters were civilians, and 34 percent of civilian casualties were children. Many casualties go unreported.

"I am Kim Phuc, the girl in the picture. My life changed forever that day. I lost two cousins and many friends in that bombing. Sixty-five percent of my body was burned, and I had to endure many surgeries. My journey into adulthood took me from Vietnam to Cuba and finally to Canada. Along the way, many people helped me. Nick Ut, the photographer who took the picture, rushed me to a hospital, saving my life. I wanted to use my experience to help others. I started the Kim Foundation, www.kimfoundation.com, to help children caught in war's crossfire by providing free medical assistance and helping them to live normal lives." The famous photograph was taken during the napalm bombing of a rural village in Vietnam in 1972.

"Volunteering makes me feel good. It makes me smile more. It makes me cry more." —Arn Chorn-Pond

As a child, Arn Chorn-Pond survived the horrors of the Khmer Rouge regime in Cambodia by playing revolutionary songs on the flute. Today he is an internationally recognized human rights leader and speaker.

War and Peace

Peace: Why cause war?
War: Because I like hurting people.
Peace: But why do you like hurting people?
War: Because I don't care about anybody.
Peace: Why don't you care about anybody?
War: Because I've been hurt too.

Jammie, 9
United States

Anti-landmine poster,
International Campaign to Ban Landmines.

One can **teach** for peace.

"I will never accept that ignorance and intolerance should hide my face ever again." —**Mehria Azizi, Afghanistan**

Mehria Azizi stood in front of her class of neighborhood girls, nervously glancing out the window to the Kabul street below. It was the same window through which a stray bullet killed her mother while she prayed. Mehria was eight. For the next five years she lived in constant fear of the Taliban terrorists who had taken control of Afghanistan. Basic freedoms were denied to females; they were forced to spend most of their time indoors, allowed out only if accompanied by a male and covered head-to-toe with a burka. Flying kites and other children's games were forbidden. Even wearing white socks became a crime. Teaching girls to read and write was punishable by death. But Mehria knew that education was very important if the Afghan population was to break the cycle of poverty and unemployment that led to the fighting. She knew her enemy was not the religious police but ignorance.

"As a journalist I can help change others' thoughts and behavior, and I can choose to portray upheaval. I choose peace." —Mehria Azizi

After the fall of the Taliban, Mehria Azizi was trained as one of Afghanistan's first camerawomen. She worked on the documentary *Afghanistan Unveiled*, which revealed how women live outside of Kabul. With a group of women, Mehria traveled through some of the most dangerous parts of the country. She has received many death threats, and her life is always in danger.

Afghani girls in school. Education is a basic right for all children, yet one in five of the developing world's two billion children are not receiving proper education. This means that another generation of illiterate children, like their parents before them, will be unable to break the cycle of poverty, disease, abuse, war and more.

"The worst thing we can do is to not do anything. I want to make a difference. I want to do something— even if it's small. I am going to raise $750 to pay for one year of a teacher's salary to educate girls like me." —Alaina Podmorow, 10, Canada

Alaina Podmorow thought it wasn't fair that many girls in Afghanistan were not able to go to school because their faith required they have female teachers. She started an organization, **Little Women 4 Little Women in Afghanistan**, to raise money through recycling, making bracelets, selling donuts and holding talent shows.

FACT: Annual spending on weapons and the military has reached US $1 trillion, or US $1.5 million a minute.[8] The cost of four stealth bombers alone would cover the cost of **four years of elementary education** for the billions of children in the world denied elementary education.[9]

"Adults have a duty to listen to children. This is our right as children—they have to listen. And if they are not abiding with that right, we will work harder to make them hear." —Om Prakash, India

Om Prakash Gurjar was five when he was taken from his parents in India, who were too poor to keep him. He was beaten and forced to work long hours with very little food before he was rescued three years later. Om enrolled in school, where he realized that education was the key to a better life. He visited schools and set up "child friendly villages." Om also helped children get birth certificates—the first step toward enshrining children's rights, proving their age and helping to protect them from exploitation, slavery, trafficking, forced marriage or serving as child soldiers. Om Prakash was awarded the **International Children's Peace Prize** in 2006.

Everyone wants peace; how do we get there? By integrating peace education into all schools!

"Education is the most powerful weapon that you can use to change the world." —Nelson Mandela, South Africa

The Feelings of a Child

My tears have shed,
My siblings are dead
I cry and cry,
Nobody cares why

But why should a gun stay held in my hand,
Why should enmity and hatred always stand?
Why can't love be given to me?
Why can't books be right in front of me?

We are the children of today,
And generations of tomorrow
We are plants today,
And will be trees tomorrow

Omar Aziz, 13
Afghanistan/Canada

Educate the Youth. Art by Sanora Silvoy.

One can **befriend** an enemy
for peace.

"In the story of the lion and the lamb, it is a child that leads the animals to lie down peacefully together. I believe children can make this world a better place. The more of us who learn to accept differences and help others, the better our world will be." **—Nickole Evans, United States**

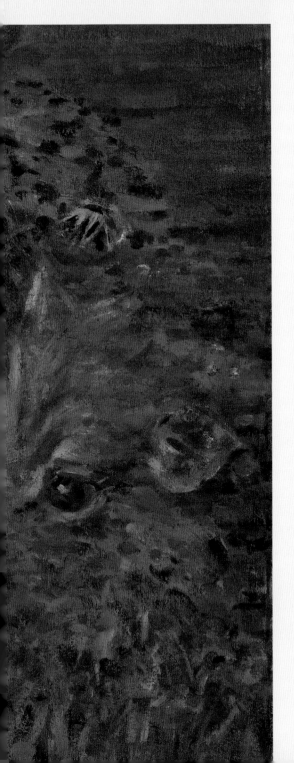

Nickole Evans heard the gunshots and her friend's screams. She turned to see two boys with BB guns run away, and then she felt a burning pain in her side. Nickole's injuries soon healed, but the ache in her heart from the violence remained. The police dealt with the boys and spoke with their parents; when Nickole saw the fear and distress of the boys' parents, she decided to visit and console them. Nickole learned that the family had recently fled to America from the war in the Balkans; the boys had grown up with guns in a place where guns and violence were normal. Nickole offered to help the family adapt peacefully to their new environment by assisting them with English, homework and computer training.

Nickole, trained in dispute resolution and peer mediation, helps teachers establish Safe Schools and provide alternatives to bullying and youth violence.

Samantha Smith, 10, United States.

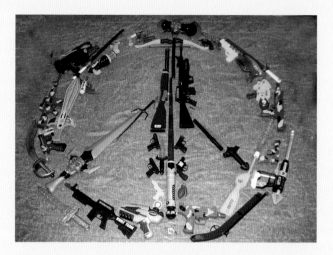

SAVE (Students Against Violence Everywhere) encourages people to buy nonviolent toys and CDs as presents. "Some of the video games I've seen that show lots of blood are really violent. Some of the kids aren't old enough to process that it's all make-believe." —Nickole Evans

A child who has lived through war has emotional scars that last a long time. Making art together made friends of children on both sides of the violent Israeli/Palestinian conflict in the Middle East. "We painted, we talked, we played. It was fun to work with them. I found out they are good." —Bar Ama, 12, Israel

In 1982, during the Cold War, Samantha Smith worried that the new Soviet leader intended to drop bombs on America. She wrote Yuri Andropov to ask him if this was true. After her letter was published in the Soviet newspaper, Samantha received an assurance from Andropov that his citizens wanted peace. He invited the Smiths to visit his country. The Soviet people greeted them with love and respect. After Samantha had made many friends, she said, *"I think Soviet and American leaders should exchange granddaughters for two weeks every year because a president wouldn't want to send a bomb to a country his granddaughter would be visiting."* Samantha Smith wrote a book about her trip, dedicated *"to the children of the world. They know that peace is always possible."*

"We normally see children with plastic machine guns pretending to kill each other, but we can teach those children that playing with a ball is much more fun.
—Mireille Karaki, Generations For Peace

Sport is a valuable tool for peace. Thousands of years ago, warring countries put aside their differences and hatred for a month-long truce to take part in the ancient Olympic Games. In recent games, archrivals have marched together under the same flag. The Beijing 2008 Olympics' program is based on a peace theme, "One world. One dream." The first Youth Olympic Games in 2010 will educate young people in the values of respect, fair play, tolerance and friendship that sports teach.

HRH Prince Feisal al-Hussein of Jordan began **Generations For Peace**, a sport initiative that brings together youth from divided communities and provides organized sport to teach teamwork and help them learn that each athlete is not an enemy but a friend who shares the same concerns, fears, worries and hopes.

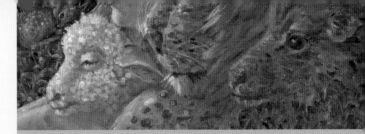

"Love is the only force capable of transforming an enemy into friend." —Martin Luther King Jr.

For Our World

In so many ways, we are the same.
Our differences are unique treasures.
We have, we are, a mosaic of gifts
To nurture, to offer, to accept.
We need to be.
Just be.
Be for a moment.
Kind and gentle, innocent and trusting,
Like children and lambs,
Never judging or vengeful
Like the judging and vengeful.
And now, let us pray,
Differently, yet together,
Before there is no earth, no life,
No chance for peace.

Mattie Stepanek wrote several books of poetry with messages of hope and peace during his brief and difficult life with muscular dystrophy. This poem was written on September 11, 2001, when Mattie was eleven years old.

FACT: Sweden and Norway have successful voluntary restriction of the sale of war toys.

One can ask, "What difference can **you** make for peace?"

See what happens when snowflakes come together...

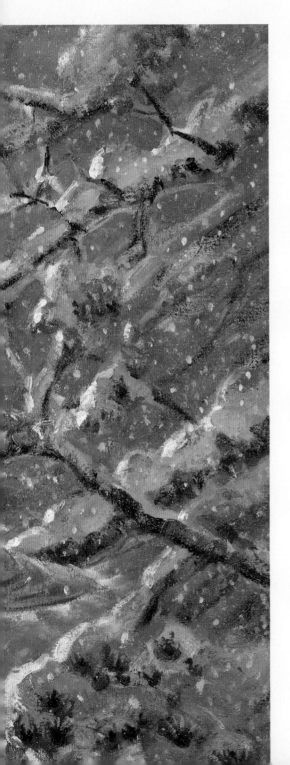

Two birds perched on a tree. A gentle sprinkling of snow fell around them.

The chickadee asked the wild dove, "How much does a snowflake weigh?"

The dove turned his attention to the delicate crystals on his feathers. "Why, nothing," he said with certainty. "Nothing at all."

The chickadee, who loved to chatter, said, "Then I have a story for you."

He began, "One day I sat on a branch of a fir tree when it began to snow. It wasn't snowing heavily, as in a raging blizzard. No, it was peaceful and dreamlike. Since I didn't have anything better to do, I decided to count the snowflakes settling on the twigs and needles of my branch.

"I counted hundreds and thousands, then hundreds of thousands. I was tired and hungry but I kept counting the snowflakes into the millions. Their number was exactly 2,890,634. When the 2,890,635th dropped onto the branch—nothing at all, as you say—the branch broke off."

The chickadee bobbed his head and flew away.

The dove, who was widely considered an authority on peace, thought about the story for a while.

"Perhaps there is only one person's voice lacking for peace to come to the world."

—*Anonymous*

43

Peace is not just the absence of war; it is the presence of fairness, justice and kindness. One act of forgiveness is an act of peace. Peace is how you solve problems with one another, respect and care for each other and our earth. Like the snowflakes on the branch, it is the little things that we can do every day that will change our world. Acting alone is difficult; together we can make the dream of peace come true.

"Be the change you wish to see in the world." —Mahatma Gandhi

ACKNOWLEDGMENTS

During one of my presentations of *In Flanders Fields** on Remembrance Day, someone asked, "We teach children about wars. Why don't we teach children about peace?" Good question! This was the beginning of a passionate pacifist's journey of a thousand steps. Along the way I stumbled, entered blind alleys and became hopelessly lost at times. Never one to avoid asking for directions, I finally arrived at my destination through the kindness of strangers and the unwavering support of loved ones.

Space does not permit me to name every person who so generously helped me with *One Peace*. This is a list of a few to whom I'm particularly grateful. I sincerely thank the activists and their families for allowing me to share their amazing stories, poetry and art. Marie Davis injected brilliant editorial advice at every plateau. Accompanying me from the beginning were my loyal and patient Callithumpians, Linda Sword, Dale Hamilton, Linda Hendry, Wendy Smith, Deb Quaile, Barb Marshall who, with Jenny Kitson, Anna Simon and Clare Henderson, read and critiqued many drafts. Subrata Ghosh and Ann Featherstone helped significantly. My partner, of this book and my life, Chris Wilson, worked with me step by step 'til journey's end. Love to you, always.

My models for the paintings were Teeka Rice, Eliana Train, Joseph, Olivia, Emilie, Adam and Christina Peloso, Manon Bourgeois, Anna Zawadski, Maya Linley, Gabriel Georgas, Tali Elkin, Emily Albrecht, Debsena Ganguly, Aditi Dey, Dipen Biswas, Rahul Nandi, Santanil and Moushree Ganguly, Jessica Michalski, Shelik Gharib and Bronwyn Webber.

Thanks to the staff of all the foundations and those who generously donated material, advice and expertise. Thanks to Orca Book Publishers, and especially Teresa Bubela for her outstanding book design.

*In Flanders Fields, the Story of the Poem by John McCrae, written by Linda Granfield, illustrated by Janet Wilson

ENDNOTES

1. *Profiling Refugees and the Role of UNHCR, 2007-2008*. The Office of the United Nations High Commissioner for Refugees—UNHCR—is the UN agency for Refugees (www.unhcr.org).
2. United Nations Children's Fund or UNICEF, is guided by the UN Convention on the Rights of the Child. UNICEF believes that the survival, protection and development of children must be a global priority (www.unicef.org).
3. *Zlata's Diary* by Zlata Filipovic. First published by UNICEF. Used by permission of Viking Penguin, a division of Penguin USA.
4. Anne Frank's diary describes the ordeal the Jewish teenager's family endured while hiding in an attic in Holland during WWII. They were found and sent to a Nazi concentration camp. Only her father survived.
5. Genocide is the planned and systematic extermination of an ethnic, racial, religious or national group.
6. The Spanish artist's mural *Guernica* protested the brutality and inhumanity of the bombing of the town of Gernika during the Spanish Civil War.
7. Costa Rica's army was abolished in 1949 after a civil war left thousands dead.
8. Stockholm International Peace Research Institute.
9. Free The Children (www.freethechildren.com).

PHOTO CREDITS

Page 4: line drawings by Janet Wilson; photo of Chechen children in a basement by photographer Peter Bouckaert, courtesy of Human Rights Watch (www.hrw.org).

Page 5: International Day of Peace dove logo: graphic courtesy of World Harmony Foundation, Mayors for Peace, Global Family, UN International Day Of Peace © the Outreach Division, United Nations Department of Public Information (www.internationaldayofpeace.org); poem courtesy of Time to Abolish War! A youth agenda for peace and justice, Hague Appeal for Peace 2000; art by Hawrah Abbas, age 5, courtesy of Claudia Lefko, Iraqi Art Exchange (www.iraqichildrensart.org).

Page 7: Zlata photo by photographer Alexandra Boulat, permission of SIPA.

Page 8: cartoon courtesy of animator Cory Wilson; photo of Darfur orphan girl with baby sister courtesy of Mia Farrow.

Page 9: photo of Darfur refugee camp courtesy of Mia Farrow; photo of Ronan Farrow courtesy of UNICEF/Shehzad Noorani; Kids' Guernica Nepal courtesy of www.kids-guernica.org; middle drawing "Janjaweed and Soldiers: Sudan," Abd al-Rahman, age 13, courtesy of Human Rights Watch; bottom drawing by Adam, courtesy of Mia Farrow.

Page 11: photo of Farlis Calle by William Torres, courtesy of UNICEF.

Page 12: photo of members of the CCMP courtesy of Lydia Smith; photo of Peace Child courtesy of Bill Roe.

Page 13: Child Art 2000 poster by Amal Al-Hajj, age 9, Yemen, courtesy of Ashfaq Ishaq, ICAF (International Child Art Foundation, www.icaf.org); photo of David Shepherd and Travis Price permission of The Chronicle Herald Library, Halifax.

Pages 15, 16 & 17: all photos courtesy of Free The Children (www.freethechildren.com).

Page 17: poster art by You Kyeong Jin, Republic of Korea, The Lions International Peace Poster contest Merit Award winner 2000-2001, courtesy of Lions Clubs International (www.lionsclubs.org).

Page 19: photo courtesy of Mr. Masahiro Sasaki and Michiko Pumpian.

Page 20: photo of The Children's Monument for Peace courtesy of photographer Robert Atendido; photo of atomic bomb courtesy of US National Nuclear Security Administration/Nevada Site Office; photo of Lennon Wall courtesy of photographer Mark Wilson, UK.

Page 21: photo of Palestinian students in Syria courtesy of Art Miles Japan; Japan/Syria mural image courtesy of Art Miles Japan; China mural image courtesy of The Art Miles Mural Project (www.the-art-miles-mural-project.org).

Pages 23 & 24: photos of Sonia Azad courtesy of Sara Azad.

Page 24: photo of protesting children by Romeo Ranoco, permission of Reuters; photo of Gandhi, 1932, by studio photographer Vithalbhai Jhaveri, permission of Gandhi Serve; photo of Gandhi children by photographer Subrata Ghosh, with the help of members of the Jhalapala theatre group: Debsena, Santanil and Moushree Ganguly, and Rahul Nandi, with models Aditi Dey and Dipen Biswas.

Page 25: photo of Charlotte Aldebron courtesy of photographer Jillian Aldebron; art by Hoimoboti Choudhury, India.

Pages 27 & 28: photos of Kimmie Weeks by photographer Hazel Chandler, courtesy of Youth Action International (www.youthactioninternational.org).

Page 28: poem courtesy of Rashid Peters, a youth peace advocate of iEARN, Sierra Leone, a non-profit global network that enables young people to use the Internet and other new technologies to engage in collaborative educational projects that both enhance learning and make a difference in the world (www.iearn.org); GuluWalk photo courtesy of Adrian Bradbury (www.guluwalk.com).

Page 29: photo of Burmese child soldier by Jeanne Hallacy; photo and lyrics courtesy of Emmanuel Jal.

Page 30: photo of Song Kosal by photographer Mette Sofie Eliseussen, courtesy of ICBL (www.icbl.org).

Page 32: photo of Kosal with Jean Chretien and Kofi Annan permission of CP Images; photo of Shoe Pyramid, Paris, 1997, by photographer Serge Pouzet, courtesy of Handicap International; photo of shoes on doormat/Austrian Campaign poster by photographer Wien Nord Pilz, courtesy of ICBL.

Page 33: art courtesy of ICBL; photo of Kim Phuc by Nick Ut, permission of CP Images; photo of Arn Chorn Pond by photographer Charley Todd, courtesy of Cambodian Living Arts (www.cambodianlivingarts.org); poem by Jammie courtesy of Kids' Guernica (www.kids-guernica.com).

Page 35: photo of Mehria Azizi by photographer Farzana Wahidy, Aina Photo.

Page 36: photo courtesy of Mehria Azizi; photo of Alaina Podmorow by photographer Jamie Podmorow (www.littlewomenforlittlewomen. com); school photo courtesy of photographer Luke Powell.

Page 37: photo of Om Prakash courtesy of Alexander Kohnstamm, Kids Rights Foundation (www.kidsrights.nl); Educate the Youth art by Sandra Silvoy, courtesy of Cristi McCabe, Roots of Peace (www.rootsofpeace.org).

Page 39: photo of Nickole Evans courtesy of Ronda Evans.

Page 40: photo of Samantha Smith by photographer Gene Willman, permission of Tass-ITAR photo agency; toys courtesy of Dean Sabatini; paintings by Ibrahim Qulaghasi (top) and Yarden Davidian (bottom) from Children of Jerusalem Painting Pain Dreaming Peace, a Project of The Institute for the Study of Religions and Communities in Israel, Ramat Hasharon, Israel courtesy of Kitty Cohen (www.folkloreoftheother.org.il).

Page 41: photo and logo courtesy of Generations For Peace (www.generationsforpeace.org); poem excerpt by Mattie Stepanek from Hope Through Heartsongs, permission of Hyperion.